THE PHILC

FOUR OBJECTIVES
OF
HUMAN LIFE

DHARMA
Right Conduct

ARTHA
Right Wealth

KAMA
Right Desire

MOKSHA
Right Exit (Liberation)

The Philosophy of Hinduism

Four Objectives of
HUMAN LIFE

DHARMA — The Right Conduct
ARTHA — The Right Wealth
KAMA — The Right Desires
MOKSHA — The Liberation
(The Right Exit)

J.M. Mehta

HINDOOLOGY
BOOKS

HINDOOLOGY
BOOKS

An imprint of
Pustak Mahal®
J-3/16 , Daryaganj, New Delhi-110002
☎ 23276539, 23272783, 23272784 • *Fax:* 011-23260518
E-mail: info@pustakmahal.com • *Website:* www.pustakmahal.com

Sale Centres

- 10-B, Netaji Subhash Marg, Daryaganj, New Delhi-110002
  ☎ 23268292, 23268293, 23279900 • *Fax:* 011-23280567
  E-mail: rapidexdelhi@indiatimes.com
  - **Hindu Pustak Bhawan**
  6686, Khari Baoli, Delhi-110006
  ☎ 23944314, 23911979

Branches

Bangaluru: ☎ 080-22234025 • *Telefax:* 080-22240209
E-mail: pustak@airtelmail.in • pustak@sancharnet.in
Mumbai: ☎ 022-22010941, 022-22053387
E-mail: rapidex@bom5.vsnl.net.in
Patna: ☎ 0612-3294193 • *Telefax:* 0612-2302719
E-mail: rapidexptn@rediffmail.com
Hyderabad: *Telefax:* 040-24737290
E-mail: pustakmahalhyd@yahoo.co.in

© **Pustak Mahal, New Delhi**

ISBN 978-81-223-0945-**4**

Edition : 2010

Printed at : Param Offsetters, Okhla, New Delhi-110020

Contents

Preface

*H*uman life is unique and offers us great opportunities to attain the highest goals of life. It has the capacity and the essential equipment which no other living creature has. That is why only in human life, the highest achievement is possible and not in any other form. However, it is indeed a pity that most human beings remain ignorant about the real purpose of their existence and hence, spend most valuable span of their lives in mundane pursuits.

An individual is born, enters childhood, grows up, get old and finally dies. During the short span of life available to us, we all eat, drink, sleep, perform activties required of us and try to be happy, as long as we live, and then die. This seems to be a sad but inevitable climax of life. Between birth and death, there is a strange mix of pleasure and pain. Sometimes, there is more pleasure and sometimes, there is more pain. In human existence, in general, there is no absolute pleasure or absolute pain; wherever there is pleasure, there is pain, as well. The great English writer, Thomas Hardy remarked that life is a general drama of pain,or suffering punctuated by an occasional episode of happiness, here and there.

We all want to be free from pain and misery of life, but either do not have the necessary knowledge to attain that freedom or do not make the requisite effort to work for it.

What is the way out then?

It is our good fortune, that our spiritual leaders called *guru, rishis*, teachers by virtue of their great spiritual effort or *sadhna* had discovered the means to achieve the above mentioned goal. In order to do that, they had laid down and standardised FOUR OBJECTIVES of life. These objectives are indeed very difficult, but not impossible. And they form the basis of Hinduism. First of all, human beings are required to equip themselves with moral values which would govern all the aspects of life—material and spiritual. These objectives have to be achieved through four human life. These four stages of life called *Ashrams* include the preparatory stage, the main dominant period of household, the retired life and the last remaining period of seclusion. The ancient Indian philosophy envisages a definite plan of action where the material and the spiritual aspects of life coalesce harmoniously for the ultimate fulfilment.

This small book, primarily deals with the above mentioned four objectives of life and allied topics. An attempt has been made to briefly explain them, in an easy manner, to enable a general reader to understand these fundamentals of human life and consequently, to live life in a useful and desirable manner.

J. M. Mehta

Human Life

Human being is at the TOP of God's creation. Human life is the greatest gift of God to an individual soul. The organic structure of body, mind and intelligence, besides other organs with which a human being is endowed, are far superior than that given to other living beings. The functions which a human can perform exceed in quality, quantity and capability, to those performed by other creatures. Human life is therefore unique in itself as compared to other living beings. To be human is a rare privilege. This fact is noteworthy while initiating any discussion about life in general and the journey of human life, in particular.

Most human beings spend their lives without bothering to know what life is all about. They have a mundane existence, doing something or the other to sustain life. They go about their daily routines, without realising the real significance of life. Earning a livelihood remains the main concern. 'Eat, drink and be merry' is the motto of their life. For them, life is for self-indulgence and is to be spent in the fulfilment of one desire or the other.

Only a few people seriously think about life, its realities, its final goal and how it should be lived in a proper manner. Various thinkers, writers and poets have described life in different ways. Depending upon their individual experiences each described life as a journey, a struggle, a play, a dream, a drama, duty, fun, fantasy, etc. It has also been thought as unreal, a force, meaningless, a hallucination, etc. Anyway, life is full of action and experiences—sweet and sour. To some, life is rosy, while to others, it is full of thorns, and so on.

According to general belief, the span between birth and death is considered life. Some people wrongly think that human life ends with death and there is only one lifespan, which is really not true. Life continues even after death in some form or the other. Death is only a doorway to another life which continues and never ceases to be. Our present span of life is only another step forward in the ongoing journey of life.

In this context, a vital question which arises here is as to how to live this life which we have been blessed with? We also wonder whether there is any goal of life and if there are any guidelines to live life and any specific objectives to be achieved during the current span of life? A common person does not seem to be aware of any satisfactory answer to these questions. In this context, it may be relevant to quote here the following story:

Once a king called the most wise philosopher of his kingdom and said to him, "I would like you to describe human life in a few simple words." The philosopher requested the king to give him one week to answer the question and the king agreed. After one week, the philosopher returned and said, "For most people, life can be described in the following words:

"He was born, he grew up, got married, begot children which he helped to grow and thereafter, he died.

In brief, life passed through different stages which include birth, childhood, youth, married or domestic life, old age and death. Birth, growth, decline and death—these few words are sufficient to sum up life. Of course, one can fill up blanks and extend the short story of life into a long tale.

Now, we must ponder over the basic issues of how to live life and how to achieve its objectives. A life without objectives is not worthy or desirable. In our worldly life, we make efforts to acquire education, adopt a profession, acquire wealth and property, get married, produce children and help them grow up in life, in a manner in which we have lived and even better than that. In living life, besides requiring wealth, property and children, we also try to achieve success, name and fame, status, honour, power and comforts of the mundane life. In this process of worldly life, a human being mainly passes through two types of experiences which are good or bad, pleasant or unpleasant. These, either give comfort and pleasure or discomfort and pain. Life may thus be described as a strange combination of pleasure and pain. In our worldly existence, nobody wants to experience pain. All human beings, and even other living beings want pleasure, but no pain. In the background of all human activities, there is an inner urge for pleasure, happiness or freedom from pain and misery. It may, therefore, be argued that the main objective of life is to attain happiness.

The question that arises here is—do we achieve happiness in life? What we may really get is a temporary relief or a transient happiness, which is not lasting. Pleasure and pain take their turns. There is a saying: 'Where there is pleasure, there is also pain.' Pleasure and pain are two sides of the same coin. When we talk of real happiness, it is the total happiness, the permanent bliss or *ananda*, i.e., freedom from all pain and misery. Do we get it? I am afraid, not. Even the richest, the most powerful men on earth were never happy completely; some of them met even tragic ends. The lives of ordinary and common people are generally full of pain, misery and unhappiness. Most of us are groping in the dark in search of happiness. Then, what is the way out? How do we attain total happiness or permanent bliss?

Our scriptures, *rishis* and saints provide guidelines in this direction. They tell us that attainment of liberation is possible by following the spiritual path. However, this final state of happiness or the ultimate goal of life cannot be attained instantly by or through some sudden miracle. A human being desires achieving the final goal of life but has to go through an arduous process. He has to accomplish certain tasks in life before he can fully qualify himself to reach the final destination. Those tasks represent the objectives which are required to be achieved in human life alone. That is why, it is most essential to make the best of the current span of life.

We shall discuss these objectives of life in the following chapters.

●●●

Four Objectives of
Human Life

According to ancient Indian philosophy, human life has a definite aim, a final goal, that is required to be achieved. This goal may be achieved, either in the current span of life or in a series of lifespans. A human being remains entangled in the vicious circle of births and deaths, until the final goal is attained. This final goal of life has been described in different ways. We may call it liberation from pain and misery; freedom from birth and death; attainment of a perfect stage of total happiness; enduring bliss or *ananda*. Some people may call it self-realisation or God-realisation. A popular word to denote the final goal of life is termed as *moksha* which in common parlance means liberation from all pain and misery. There could be no better goal of life than this. This is the highest achievement, the last desirable destination, the final goal of human life.

Now the question arises, how to achieve the final goal of life? In this material world, there are several smaller objectives or aims to be achieved. One has to make a lot of efforts to achieve those objectives. For instance, one has to be steady, gain knowledge to complete education and then, one has to work hard, adopt a profession, and be successful in one's career. Earning one's livelihood requires lot of efforts. Similarly, acquisition of wealth, property and other comforts of life demand hard work and continuous struggle. A human being has to go through a long and arduous path in order to achieve material wealth, name and fame, excellence in professional field, status, success and power, and so on. These mundane achievements which we attain in the material world are insignificant in comparison with the highest goal of life. One can therefore, imagine how much harder one may have to work to achieve that goal.

The achievement of the final goal of life requires fulfilment of certain objectives or obligations. One has to cross many milestones before the final destination is reached. Even in the material world, one has to acquire certain capabilities or meet particular standards, before one can achieve a desired target or objective of life. One has to meet higher standards and follow a rigorous disciplined life to achieve the goal in the spiritual domain, where the path is much more difficult, and the efforts required far more arduous. The attainment of the spiritual goal cannot be made possible in an instant or by some strange miracle of God. There has to be a well laid out path, a definite plan to achieve the goal. On the basis of their knowledge gained through the highest spiritual pursuits (*sadhna*), the ancient Indian sages (called the *rishis*) had discovered a plan of life to achieve the final goal of life. Accordingly, they had standardised certain OBJECTIVES of human life, for the guidance of all mankind. There are 'FOUR OBJECTIVES OF HUMAN LIFE', by following which, the highest goal of life can be achieved. These four objectives are as follows:

1. DHARMA – The religion or righteousness through right conduct.
2. ARTHA – Acquisition of wealth and its proper use.
3. KAMA – Fulfilment of noble desires.
4. MOKSHA – Liberation or the final goal.

It is essential to have a correct understanding of the above three objectives and to fulfil them, before the final objective can be achieved. Our present span of life is the duration between birth and death. During this lifespan, one is mainly pre-occupied with fulfilment of all sorts of desires arising in everyday life. Hence, there is the necessity of Artha or wealth. Thus, acquisition of wealth and its use in the fulfilment of numerous desires of life becomes the most important activities of human life. In order to meet these requirements, activity or desires of life in a proper and worthy manner, it is essential to regulate them under certain proper principles based on moral values. It is here that the role of Dharma is called for. It is therefore, utmost essential to understand and practise Dharma, while following the objectives of Artha and Kama and thus, pave the way for Moksha.

By following the above mentioned objectives, an individual can achieve the final goal of life in a single span of life or through a series of lifespans, depending upon the quality of efforts made earnestly, dedication and devotion, etc. of the aspirant.

We shall describe these objectives in some detail in the following chapters.

●●

Dharma (True Religion)

Of the four objectives of life, *Dharma* is the first and the foremost. Broadly speaking, *Dharma* may be considered synonymous with true religion or righteousness. It is the primary means, tool or equipment which is required to be used in all walks of human existence. It is therefore utmost important to grasp the true meaning of *Dharma* in order to implement its significance in all aspects and in order to achieve other objectives. It is impossible to achieve the final goal of life without practising it, and that is why it occupies a prominent position.

Let us, therefore, try to understand and explain the true meaning of *Dharma,* which is basically a Sanskrit word (धर्म) and has been derived from its root *Dhri* (धृ) which means to 'uphold', to 'adopt', to 'safeguard', etc. In essence, *Dharma,* therefore means that which is worthy of practising, and following, and also which binds or safeguards. According to the *Vedic* philosophy, *Dharma* is a comprehensive term which covers an entire range of values. It stands for a collective value system of our ancient spiritual heritage. As such, it has far greater significance than the present day conventional or sectarian term of religion. Thus *Dharma,* or true religion, not merely specifies the spiritual and moral disciplines, but also develops a healthy and happy social form based on moral conduct and value system. It is not merely a path of worship and religious rituals, or a means to some specified worldly mission, or for fulfilment of mundane desires. In reality, it implies observance of those principles which bind human beings together not only for the pursuit of an ideal goal of life, but also with desirable and noble social pursuits and accomplishment. In this manner, *Dharma* as a socio-ethical doctrine, which when practised in the right spirit, regulates a disciplined, healthy, happy, beneficial and peaceful living. It is a blueprint for making an ideal individual and the most beneficial way of life.

The Sanskrit word *Dharma* has no exact equivalent in the English language. It has much wider significance than the word 'Religion' in its ordinary sense or in the conventional form currently in vogue. While *Dharma* is one and the same for the entire mankind, the prevalent concept of religion divides mankind into different sects having their different modes of worship, rituals, traditions, customs and festivals and even different prophets and religious preachers, leaders and so on.

Before considering the meaning of *Dharma* from some other angles, let us first examine the prevailing concept and the current scenario of the practice of religion in the present day world. When we talk of religion in the existing context, names of several present-day conventional religions crop up in our mind. These include Christianity, Islam, Hinduism, Buddhism, Jainism etc. Most of these religions started at a certain time in human history and were founded or propagated by some spritual leaders. Each of these religions has its own holy book containing its teachings, besides modes of worship, religious plans, rituals, traditions and customs etc. Thus Christianity was founded by Jesus Christ and their holy book is the Bible, Islam was founded by Prophet Muhammad and the Quran is their most sacred book. Similarly, Buddhism, Jainism, Sikhism and some other smaller sects have their own respective founders and separate holy books. Hinduism has many gods including Lord Rama and Lord Krishna, besides several other saints and holy men, and it also has several holy books which include the Vedas, the Gita, the Ramayana, besides other holy texts and spiritual treatises. But Hinduism is perhaps the most unique of all the religions. In the strict conventional term it is not religion as such, because it was not founded by any specific religion leader. It has been described by scholars as 'a way of life'. The word 'Hindu' has its origin in the word 'Sindhu'. When foreign invaders came to India and reached up to the river Sindhu, those who lived across this river were named by them as **Sindhus** which later on got changed into **Hindus**. It is therefore, inferred that the religion of Hindus, or in other words Hinduism was associated with the people of India. In fact, Hinduism now being practised in its different forms has evolved from the ancient Indian religion which was based on the philosophy of the *Vedas* and it may be well termed as *Vedic Dharma* or simply *Dharma*. Later on, with the passage of time, several political and social developments took place and this ancient concept of *Dharma* was interpreted and reinterpreted by differant scholars and took on new religious teachers; forms and shapes like a banyan tree which has several branches. In a way, we may say that the present form of Hinduism is a on altered form of the ancient Vedic religion.

As mentioned above, different religions which we see today, have been associated with different holy personalities or their founders. However, this does not mean that prior to their arrivals, there was no religion at all. The concept of *Dharma* was all along there, before the origin of Islam or Christianity. *Dharma,* or if we may equate it with religion in its broad and true sense, was always there and will remain at all times. Its meaning transcends the limitations imposed by the conventional religions which were established by particular founders. In a sense, perhaps, these prophets and founders also did not start something new but re-discovered values which always existed, but people had deviated due to their ignorance. They, therefore, were noted as path-finders, guides and leaders to show the path which was already there.

Let us examine further as to what are the other views regarding *Dharma*.

It is believed that when God created this universe, He is supposed to have assigned certain specific duties or functions to be performed by Nature and its derivatives. These duties or tasks which are required to be performed by them constitute their *Dharma*. Thus, *Dharma* is the performance of the role assigned to them; it is the functioning aspect governed by the unwritten law of God, which forms the essence of their existence. Therefore, the *Dharma* of something is the law of its being. We may explain the point by giving some examples, as follows:

Water flows and produces coolness. What makes water flow and to perform this function is its *Dharma*. In other words, the performance of such essential acts, as are linked with water, may be termed as its *Dharma*. Similarly, fire produces heat and light and this is its *Dharma*. Plants and trees give shade, and this is their

Dharma. Now, we cannot call these material objects as *dharmik* or religious. In these cases, *Dharma* indicates the innate qualities which they possess and perform.

In the light of the above context it may well be argued that *Dharma,* which we are discussing in relation to human life, deals with human beings and human society and therefore, it has different implications. *Dharma* owes its origin to God and is linked with human beings' moral and social values. Thus, only human beings can be called *dharmik* or religious. We do not call a dog or a donkey as being religious; it is the privilege of only human beings, who are at the top of God's creation. This is because only human beings are endowed with the necessary equipments with which they can practise *Dharma* or true religion while animals and plants are deprived. It is, however, ironical that sometimes human beings indulge in heinous acts far worse than those performed by wild animals and it is indeed tragic and paradoxical that those acts are performed in the name of religion. Terrorism being perpetrated worldwide on innocent people including women and small children is a burning example in this case.

In view of what has been stated in the previous paras, *Dharma* may be defined as the unfolding of the reality or the essence of the functioning aspect of a thing. In the context of human beings, the essential nature which makes a person worthy of being called a human—far above the level of an animal, may be construed as *Dharma*. It therefore, follows that true religion has a moral basis. It is pure, godly and divine. It is the permanent factor in human nature, without which it would remain disturbed and restless.

Dharma, as a true religion is the ideal way of life. It consists of the essential moral concepts which are to be adopted and practised in real life. A philosopher has rightly defined *Dharma* as 'Pure Action'. It is thus the moral path or way of life, by following which one acquires right knowledge that leads to God. It is the righteous endeavour to know, understand and practise the reality of truth. It is the good moral conduct, free from injustice, particularly in any form. It is a means of reforming one's present life, and for laying a firm foundation for the future destiny. This golden opportunity to sanctify this life and the future life rests only with human beings, as they are blessed with power to think, analyse, discriminate and implement right throughts into appropriate actions. Other living creatures are incapable of performing such functions. That is why, it is observed that human life is a unique opportunity and a human being is at the top of God's creation. But this highest status is possible only with the practice of *Dharma* or true religion without which a human being would become worse than even an animal. *Dharma* is thus a means for a human being to become a pure and pious person and a useful individual in society.

There is another way of looking at *Dharma* as true religion. Every person has to perform some action in life, as assigned to him by the incidence of birth or circumstances, his own choice, effort or destiny. Thus, one may have to perform his duty in accordance with his profession, status in the family or society, or by any other given situation. On this basis, *Dharma* may be defined as doing one's duty honestly, sincerely and without any selfish motive, in a just and impartial manner. *Dharma,* as such is the performance of one's duty with right attitude and proper understanding so that it makes life righteous, worth-living, secure and pure in all respects.

Dharma has to be centred in God and godliness, as all noble qualities, moral values emanate from God, who is the source of all true knowledge. It implies obedience to God's teachings, as enshrined in His attributes, as far as possible. Scriptures, if rightly interpreted can also provide necessary guidelines, besides the teachings of genuine holymen, saints and scholars. As God is one and the same for all His creations, it follows that the religion based on God and godliness is also one and the same for all mankind. Such a religion may rightly be called as *Manav Dharma* or the religion of mankind. However, in actual practice, it does not appear to be so, as different religions and sects are being followed in the world based on different teachings of various prophets, saints, religious teachers and sacred books. This has happened because the followers of different religions have interpreted their teachings in their own way, either due to ignorance or their selfish motives. In case, fundamental teachings of various faiths are interpreted in a broad sense and analysed properly, these might revolve round the following two fundamentals:

1. Genuine faith in God.

2. Practice of righteousness.

The above two basic principles could be the unifying factors for all religions. According to **Atharva Veda,** *Dharma* represents the fundamentals of true religion, the ideal form of conduct, which is the foundation of righteous living. It constitutes the basic moral principles, which uphold the society.

However, in the actual practice of worldly attainments, the following two aspects of religion are observed:

(i) **EXTERNAL:** These consist of religious forms, practices and rituals which are visible. These include, inter alia, places of worship, modes of worship, religious books, and rituals, dress code and even foods and food habits, and ways of greeting and salutations, etc. Thus we have temples, churches, mosques, gurudwaras and other forms of religious places, statues, symbols, stones and even trees and rivers, etc. We also have different holy books, e.g. the Bible, the Vedas, the Quran, Guru Granth Sahib, the Gita and several others as well. These religious sects also have their different religious symbols, signs, dresses, flags, social customs and festivals, etc.

(ii) **INTERNAL:** Different facets of religion involving deep thinking, concentration, meditation etc. *Dhyana, Dharana* and *Samadhi* of the Ashtang Yoga of Maharishi Patanjali are prominent examples of the internal aspect of religion. Silent prayer and mental *japa* also fall in the same category. These are individual activities which relate to the inner self which when practised sincerely and devotedly lead to spiritual progress and God-realisation.

As mentioned earlier, *Dharma* or true religion is an ideal way of living life, where a set of specific moral values have to be practised in thought, word and deed. The ancient Indian philosopher and law-giver,

Maharishi Manu has codified their moral values which may be briefly described as follows:

1. FORBEARANCE: This is the quality which builds power of endurance in adverse circumstances and helps a person keep his cool and remain calm and composed even in the face of hardships. This moral virtue enables a person to face all the difficult situations of life with patience and wisdom.

2. CONTROL OF MIND: The mind is restless and ever changing. It is always engaged in some thought process and the fluctuations of mind travel with the fastest speed. Life would not function normally if the mind remains tense and restless. It is therefore necessary to control the mind and make it peaceful. This can be made possible through constant practice, proper understanding and non-attachment. Logical thinking, right actions, practice of meditation, engagement in noble activities and constant remembrance of God help to make the mind consistent. For example, regular practice of Pranayam (regulation of breath) is a sure means to control the mind.

3. FORGIVENESS: There is a popular saying, 'To err is human, to forgive divine.' It is quite difficult to exercise this moral virtue in an atmosphere of hatred and jealousy in human relationships. One has to be physically and morally strong to practise this quality. A righteous and weak person wronged by a powerful sinner cannot grant pardon to the latter. It is also not advisable to forgive a habitual wrongdoer and an evil-minded person as far as possible.

4. NON-STEALING: This moral virtue involves absence of greed. One should not take away or acquire anything which does not belong to onself, without paying proper price and without the permission of the rightful owner.

5. CLEANLINESS: This includes both external and internal aspects. Thus, the body, physical environment and the mind should be kept clean and pure. While it is easy to keep our body and the external environment clean with water and cleaning material, it is much more difficult to keep the mind clean and pure. The motto in everyday life and behaviour should be—'See no evil, hear no evil and do no evil.'

6. CONTROL OF SENSES: These are the five senses of knowledge and the five senses of action. When these senses come in contact with the external world, attachment and desires are produced. Desires, if not kept under check, lead to evil consequences. One should never be a slave to those senses but be their master.

7. **WISDOM:** One should acquire wisdom through right knowledge, as enshrined in religious books, scriptures and other good literature. Experience is also a great teacher. One should also learn from one's own experience, as well as from the experience of others. Past mistakes should not be repeated. One can also learn from good company and by listening to sermons and discourses.

8. KNOWLEDGE: One should acquire knowledge of both material and spiritual world. Right knowledge, proper understanding, and utilisation of that knowledge, are useful for our present and future lives. Piety, steadfastness and hard work are necessary for acquiring right knowledge. Study of good literature, guidance of competent teachers, good company and self effort are some of the important means of acquiring knowledge.

9. TRUTH: One must practise truth in thought, word and deed. A truthful behaviour is essential for a truly religious life.

10. NON-ANGER: One should remain calm and balanced in the face of provocation. Anger not only hurts others but also causes damage to the angry person. It is, therefore, necessary to exercise patience and restraint to avoid and control anger. Non-anger leads to peace of mind which is essential for the practitioner of a religious life.

The above qualities, by and large, cover all aspects of our physical and mental life. Spiritual practices, like meditation, pranayam and attending of spiritual discourses and congregations help in the process of making our life truly religious. In case a person finds some other useful activity, from his personal experience, the same may also be put into practice. It may be emphasised here that the practice of *Dharma* or true religion lies in our conduct, based on moral values and qualities and not in the following of some old traditions and rituals which are based on ignorance and blind faith.

On the basis of various philosophical thoughts and views expressed in relation to *Dharma,* it may be worthwhile to define it in the following different ways:

i.   *Dharma* consists of the observance of those laws and performance of those duties which uphold the society and the whole creation.

ii. It involves the practice of moral values by following which an individual attains both material and spiritual progress and welfare.

iii. The innate quality or the functioning basis of a particular thing is its *Dharma*.

iv. To follow rightly the basic principles enshrined in our scriptures is *Dharma*.

v. The practice of ten or eleven virtues as prescribed by Maharishi Manu, supported by other holy persons and endorsed by our scriptures constitutes *Dharma*.

vi. It is also doing one's duty honestly, sincerely and without selfish attachment.

vii. *Dharma* may be defined as 'Pure Action'.

viii. It is the unfolding of the reality of essential, intrinsic human nature, which in other words is 'Godliness'.

ix. It is the performance of the role assigned by God to Nature and its derivatives, in accordance with the divine laws.

The above list may not be exhaustive and there may also be some other manner of defining *Dharma*.

The above definitions and earlier discussions on *Dharma* make it amply clear that the essence of *Dharma* lies in the moral conduct or the practice of virtues in real life and not mere conventional rituals and practices followed by different religious sects on the basis of their beliefs.

In conclusion, if we have to define *Dharma* or true religion in one sentence, it may be as follows:

'*Dharma* or True Religion is impartial conduct, based on Truth and Justice'. It may also be defined in other words as follows:

'*Dharma* is the ideal form of conduct which builds the foundation for a right living'.

Role of Dharma

The practice of *Dharma* is most essential in all aspects of our life. There can be no right progress without *Dharma*. *Dharma* or True Religion and Righteousness are synonymous terms. One has to practise the principles of *Dharma* in thought, word and deed. There is no scope for hypocrisy here. *Dharma* can build an individual's character and good character leads to a healthy society. It can uplift individuals and through them the whole society. Thus, it can lead to peace and progress, harmony and prosperity for all mankind.

What is happening today is due to lack of implementation of a moral code of conduct, individuals are going astray in the society. Consequently, there is deception and dishonesty, injustice, greed, anger, selfishness and violence—all of which lead to chaotic conditions in the society. In case people follow the principles of *Dharma*, they will become fully conscious of right and wrong and there will be no evil anywhere in the world.

These days, there is much talk of keeping religion away from politics. This is because *Dharma* or true religion is neither being properly understood nor followed.

It is the narrow view of religion, the sectarian or conventional form of religion based on ignorance and wrong beliefs, which should be kept away or discarded, while *Dharma* or true religion must be followed.

In fact, *Dharma* should form the basis of all politics, economics and social interaction. If this is done, there will be no dirty politics, dishonesty in public life, political scandals and other evil practices which are now prevailing and spoiling our society.

In short, *Dharma* should be the very foundation of human life and activities, as it is the key to human welfare. It is the best possession of a human being. A man without it is worse than an animal; it is the foundation of culture and civilisation. *Dharma* is the only friend which accompanies the self or the soul, even after death, while all other friends and material possessions are left behind.

It is said that 'age destroys youth, disease destroys body, death, destroys physical existence, but nothing destroys *Dharma*'.

The value and importance of *Dharma* in human life and society cannot be overestimated.

In case human beings practise religion on the basis of the conclusion drawn till now religion will be a uniting factor and not a divisive force. There will then be no separate sectarian religions and there will be no Hindus, Muslims, Christians, etc. All will be human beings and there will be only one religion of all mankind, which we may perhaps call as *Manav Dharma*. This concept of true religion of *Dharma* can bring love, peace and harmony in the world.

The Current
Religious Scenario

Religion, as is commonly understood by the vast majority and prevalent in various parts of our country, has a narrow, communal and more or less, misguided approach. It is being practised in the form of separate, specified modes of worship, rituals, dogmas and traditions. It seems that people have forgotten that there is one religion, one God and one mankind. In practising different religions, we do not see human beings as the homogeneous creation of the One and the same Creator or the Universal Power, but as from different and perhaps, even conflicting sources. That is why, there are different types of followers such as Hindus, Muslims, Christians, Sikhs etc. engaged in the promotion of separate religions. Even one and the same Universal Power, which we call God or the Almighty, seems to have been bifurcated into separate versions, under different names, shapes and forms. Some gullible followers of different religions actually believe that God of their religion is different from God of other religions.

Some stick to only one or two names as prescribed in their holy books, while others may have several names of the same entity.

Due to the erroneous views of religion and God, we find that one and the same universal *Dharma* or True Religion has been divided and further sub-divided into several sects by different followers. As a result of their man-made division and due to their inherent differences, there remains a constant conflict among these sects. Such narrow and sectarian view of religion acts as a divisive force which generates hatred amidst humanity, causing riots, brutal killings, conflicts, terrorism and even wars. The practice of religion in a narrow, sectarian and parochial form can lead to untold misery and the human history is replete with several cruel and barbarous examples. Terrorism prevalent in various forms in different parts of the present day world is a grim reminder of religious ignorance and intolerance. These practices performed in the name of religion are acts of foolishness and not of religion.

Even in the present day modern world, numerous, erroneous, misleading and harmful practices are being followed under the garb of religion. Such practices are being followed in our country by a large number of illiterate and semi-literate people. We may mention here some of the glaring practices. One such most popular example is bathing in rivers on certain occasions with the belief that all the sins committed in the past will be washed away in an instant by taking one or more dips in the holy river. Some people offer sacrifices of animals and even human beings for appeasement or oblation to gods. Some prevalent religious practices include visiting certain specified places of worship and pilgrimage, non-stop reading or reciting from certain holy books, blind faith in certain rituals, beliefs, modes of worship, holy men, idols and even some trees, religious books, buildings, hill-tops, rivers, etc. Some religions include a particular dress code and wearing of certain symbols, annual pilgrimages, etc. There may be several other unknown and mysterious religious rituals and practices being followed by different people in different parts of the world in the name of religion. However, it is not our intention to dwell on these practices in details here in this book. Our main aim here is to explain as far as possible, the correct meaning and form of *Dharma* or True Religion, which we have already done in a comprehensive manner.

We may once again emphasise that it is essential to understand true religion and practise it in the right manner, and spirit as the ideal form of conduct forms the foundation of right and peaceful living. It should always be remembered that religion is for human welfare, social welfare and for the welfare of all mankind. It should aim at a good, virtuous and blissful life for all creations.

●●

Artha (Wealth)

Artha or acquisition of wealth is the second most important pursuit or objective of human life. It is placed next to *Dharma*. It implies that the acquisition of wealth has to be based on *Dharma* or moral values. Possession of wealth is essential but observance of *Dharma* should take the first priority. It is better to be righteous and poor than to be wealthy through unfair and dishonest means.

The meaning and scope of *Artha* or wealth as enunciated by Hindu religious texts are as follows:

I. Knowledge

It has been described as the greatest wealth as nothing can be achieved without knowledge. Knowledge has been compared with light which removes darkness. It removes ignorance. Broadly speaking, knowledge may be divided into following two categories:

i.   Material knowledge which relates to matter and all material objects, arts and sciences. It includes all knowledge which relates to our daily life, the external world and its activities.

ii. Spiritual knowledge deals with our inner life, individual soul, the supreme soul and the related activities.

Material knowledge is necessary to run the chores of daily life, to understand the properties, functions and benefits of material objects and to achieve success in the external world. It forms the basis of all material development and progress. The development and survival of human life is based upon such knowledge and its proper use. Material knowledge can be gained through formal or informal education, intellectual pursuits, study of arts and sciences, etc.

Spiritual knowledge, on the other hand, is much more difficult to acquire. It needs the practice of much more tougher discipline in all aspects of life. Such knowledge can lead to the attainment of the highest goal of life, which is self-realisation or God-realisation. Acquisition of spiritual knowledge involves a long and difficult process. It can be attained through self-control, self-study and analysis, right understanding, company of holy persons, yogic *sadhna*, self-surrender, sincere devotion and the grace of God. A single span of life may not be sufficient to acquire such true knowledge; it may be possible to attain it through a series of devoted lifespans.

II. Material Wealth

Material wealth includes money, jewellery and other movable and immovable material possessions. Money is the basis of all material wealth, as it can buy all these objects. It is, therefore, the most sought after commodity with which a person can purchase most of the requirements of his life. Food, dress, house or property are the three main requirements of life and we need money to get these. Other items for which we need money include transport, travel, entertainment, education, medical treatment and so on. The general view is that—'Money can buy everything, even human beings'. There is a saying—'Money makes the mare go.' We often hear, 'There is no life without money', such is the importance of money in human life.

While money can provide for material objects and can buy comforts of life, it still cannot buy peace of mind and inner happiness. It is seen in real life that most of the rich people remain mentally disturbed and suffer from depression, worries and allied problems. A wealthy person, suffering from an incurable disease like Cancer or AIDS can buy the costliest medicines but cannot ensure a cure.

Again, a wealthy childless couple may not be able to produce a child of their own in spite of their wealth and the best available treatment. There are many more examples to add. Material wealth is thus essential, but it is not the *be all* and *end all* of human life.

III. Health

Health is a different type of wealth. There is a popular saying, 'Health is Wealth'. In order to be healthy, one has to acquire the knowledge of the ways and means of keeping fit and healthy. Again, good health depends upon the right kind of food for which money is needed. Health does not merely mean physical health; it also includes emotional and mental health. Actually, the body, mind and soul are related so all these have to be kept healthy. Good food, proper regular exercise and good thoughts are some of the fundamentals of good health. Phyisical health is surely better than material wealth. An old, wealthy person suffering from an incurable disease cannot buy health and cure, but a poor strong and healthy person can create wealth with his efforts and hard labour.

While material wealth and health are both necessary requirements of life, the wealth of knowledge is far superior and more essential, as it can produce both wealth and health.

IV. Contentment

It is said that contentment is the greatest wealth, and is different from material wealth and health.

Contentment means the absence of desire to possess more and more. It implies that one should work honestly and be satisfied with the result of his efforts.

Contentment also implies absence of feverish excitement and activity to compete with others in order to acquire more and then get caught up in a mad, unending race. The wealth of contentment is not like material wealth; it is a state of mind, it is the inner mental poise and does not depend upon external factors. It is an attitude of mind and has to be inculcated through a gradual but continuous process. The mental poise or the equanimity of mind which comes with such an attitude leads to contentment. It is, therefore, a glad acceptance of what comes to us, by circumstance or by providence, in spite of our best efforts. The attitude of contentment helps in developing a cheerful mind; it elevates a person above selfish limitations and gives him mental peace and moral strength. It is a positive condition for perpetual joy of existence. What greater wealth than this would any person need to acquire?

ROLE OF MATERIAL WEALTH

We have earlier briefly mentioned various types and sources of wealth. In the material world, where we actually live, material wealth plays a very important role in the life of an individual, as well as the society. In daily life, it runs the drama of human existence. In view of its utility and the significant role it plays in life, every individual, barring a few, wants more wealth. There is a feverish activity, a mad race, a vicious competition to acquire material wealth. Such an insatiable desire to have more and more wealth often leads to disastrous consequences such as litigation, murders, scandals and so on. That is why, it is necessary to regulate the acquisition of wealth through a proper control of moral values. This can be done only through the observance of *Dharma* which teaches selflessness and a just behaviour based on truth. Based on the philosophy of *Dharma* or true religion, we must keep in view certain basic moral principles in the process of earning, accumulating and using material wealth. Some of these principles may be mentioned as follows:

i.   Wealth should be earned through fair means. The motto, 'Honesty is the best policy' should be followed in all monetary transactions.

ii. Wealth should not be accumulated far in excess of one's requirements. A proper limit should be exercised remembering that 'Excess of everything is bad'.

iii. It should be kept in mind that wealth carved through just means leads to welfare, while wealth acquired through foul and deceptive means leads to evil consequences.

iv. One should not feel excited or intoxicated by wealth. It should not be a source of false pride, violence and unjust behaviour.

v. Wealth should be utilised to fulfil genuine needs and not for unlimited desires, as desires, are insatiable and these lead to greed and destruction.

vi. Wealth should be retained within desirable limits, as unlimited wealth leads to misuse and wastage.

vii. Surplus money should be utilised for good causes, eg. donations to the needy, underprivileged, deserving people and charitable organisations.

The above list is only indicative and not exhaustive; more such examples can be added through personal experience. While money is one of the most prized possessions of human life, it cannot buy everything as is illustrated from the following phrases:

MONEY can buy a house, but not a happy home.

can buy a soft bed, but not sound sleep.

can buy you company but not true friendship.

can buy medicines, but not good health.

can buy comfort, but not peace of mind.

can buy good food, but not good appetite.

can buy entertainment, but not happiness.

Money can buy you lots of things, but not Everything.

It may be concluded from the above lines that while money can play a very useful role in the acquisition of several utilities of life, yet it has several limitations. It, therefore, cannot offer a complete package to live life.

While it is essential to acquire material wealth, it is utmost important that it must be acquired through just and fair means.

The principles of truth, fair means and hardwork must be kept in mind and actually practised while procuring wealth. Laws of *Dharma* or righteousness should govern the process of acquisition and expenditure of wealth. A truly religious person will not use any dishonest method to earn money. Thus, acquisition of wealth through deception, fraud, stealing, bribes and any other foul means is not permissible under the principles of true religion.

In a society where acquisition of wealth is regulated through righteous means, or the rules of *Dharma*, there will be no corruption, injustice, foul play or unwanted litigation. Peace and harmony will prevail in such a society which in turn would be free from theft, robbery and murders arising from greed for the acquisition of wealth. Let us remember what the great Indian thinker Chanakya has said:

> *"Wealth which is procured through just and truthful means is WORTHY."*

Another philosopher has said:

"'Money obtained by wrong means will disappear bit by bit; money earned bit by bit, by right means, will grow and grow."

Greed plays an important role in the desire to acquire more material wealth. Let us see what Mahatma Gandhi said about it:

> *"The world is enough for everyone's needs but not ever enough for one man's greed."*

Greed for material wealth is insatiable. Acquisition of wealth must be kept within a proper limit, as its accumulation produces a sort of harmful intoxication and false pride. It leads to the bolstering of one's ego. A wealthy person may not care for the opinion and feelings of other persons. Wealthy people often love and lead a life of luxury and unnecessary indulgence and gratification of senses. Since they have surplus money, they can afford to spend on lavish eating and drinking and on acquisition of material objects just to flaunt their wealth. These days, lakhs of rupees are unnecessarily spent on ostentatious celebrations of marriages, birthday bashes and other so-called social parties and functions. While excess of wealth can lead to evil practices, abuse of wealth can lead to bad habits, drug addiction, drinking, gambling, prostitution, etc. Thus, such money, which is spent on unnecessary celebrations, undesirable pastimes and acquisition of non-essential possessions like jewellery, costly watches, expensive cars and dresses, etc can very well be utilised for the welfare of the poor and the underprivileged people of the society.

A person who becomes crazy about wealth becomes more and more greedy. A story about a greedy king who was very fond of accumulating gold, runs as follows:

A king was very fond of gold- so much so that even doors of his palace had golden coverings. He a had lot of gold but still his hunger for gold was not satisfied. So he prayed to God, with full devotion, for a very long time. After some time, God was impressed and told him to ask for a boon. The king was overjoyed and he requested God, "Kindly grant me that power, by which, whatever I touch should turn into gold." God said, "So be it", and the king got that power. He was extremely happy but his happiness was only short-lived.

When the king returned to his palace, he touched a stone and it became all gold. He was so excited that he went on touching whatever came his way. In this manner, all his furniture and other wares became gold and he was mad with joy. He called for food and drinks but when he touched these, they all became gold. He could not eat or drink and became very helpless. He had a small daughter whom he loved very much. When she came to him, he touched her and she too turned into a lifeless statue of gold. At this happening, the king felt extremely miserable. He, therefore, again prayed to God and requested Him to withdraw his boon. He wept bitterly and apologised for his greed. God took pity on the king and withdrew his boon. So, all the things came to their original position; his lovely daughter became alive and he could now eat and drink. In this way, the greedy king learnt a lesson and never gave in to greed again. He distributed all his excess wealth among the poor and the needy people.

The above story has a moral that greed for more and more leads to disaster and wealth should be kept within a desirable limit. While we must earn wealth as it is essential for a living, our aim should be to keep it within a proper limit and to earn it through righteous means. All surplus wealth must be distributed among the needy or utilised for righteous and charitable purposes. One must remember that 'contentment is the greatest wealth'. We should practise contentment which should be our ideal in the matter of acquisition and utilisation of wealth or *Artha*.

In short, while material wealth is an essential requirement for living a good life, it should not be made the sole object of living. Need, and not greed, should be kept in view. Wealth should be procured through fair and just practices and used properly for the healthy, happy and purposeful maintenance of life. It should also act as a means to attain the higher aims of life. One should not be greedy and a slave of wealth, but be a master of it.

Material wealth should be used for noble causes which include helping the needy and others suffering from pain and misery. The best use of wealth is possible only by observing the principles of *Dharma* which should govern all acquisition and expenditure of wealth.

●●

Kama
(Fulfilment of Desires)

Kama is the third pursuit or objective of life. It involves sexual gratification and fulfilment of wordly desires. It is born out of attraction and attachment at the physical and mental levels. A person may be attracted to a beautiful woman, an expensive object, the glitter of gold, or some similar quality of other objects and consequently, have a desire to possess it or use it.

In a limited sense, *Kama* involves the desire for the satisfaction of sensual urges in which sexual gratification occupies a prime position. On a wider scale, it includes fulfilment of all material desires.

The sight of a beautiful girl may produce sensual excitement, physical attraction leading to feelings of love and desire for sexual gratification. Human body produces certain fluids which tend to flow out through sexual organs, at a certain age of physical development. This phenomenon produces a natural urge for sexual gratification, which then becomes a physical and emotional necessity. However, it is utmost essential that urges born out of *Kama* should be properly regulated. Without such regulation and control, these can create havoc in an individual's life and society. While the suppression of a sexual urge may prove harmful to the body, its unregulated abuse may lead to worse consequences, such as rapes and even murders. Such unsocial incidents have become everyday happenings in our modern day world.

It is our good fortune that Indian saints and philosophers had found out ways and means to control and regulate the urges arising out of *Kama*. They had devised a systematic plan of life which divides human life into four segments known as *Ashrams*. Each *Ashram* is a period of life when good qualities are supposed to be acquired in order to perform noble deeds through hard work.

We shall describe the working of these four segments of life in a separate chapter on 'Ashram Set-up'.

Fulfilment of Desires

The wider aspect of *Kama* deals with general worldly desires. Desires act as catalytic agents for action in life. There is hardly anyone who is free from desires.

Even saints who have no worldly desires have intense desire to reach God. But uncontrolled desires can lead to destruction. The Gita deals with this topic in verses 62 and 63 of Chapter II, as follows:

Verse 62

When a man dwells in his mind, on the objects of senses, attachment to them is produced. From attachment springs desire, and from desire comes anger.

Verse 63

From anger arises bewilderment, and from bewilderment, loss of memory and the destruction of intelligence, and from the destruction of intelligence, he perishes.

The above verses indicate how desires are born and how they can lead to total destruction. Thus, the source of *Kama* is a passionate feeling born out of attachment to some object. It is generally noted that desires are unsatiable and satisfaction of one desire leads to more desires.

In case a desire remains unsatisfied, then anger is produced, and anger destroys the sense of discrimination, leading to total disaster. Thus *Kama* is a double-edged weapon.

Some people believe in the enjoyment of the object of desire in order to attain satisfaction, but this purpose is never attained. Like fire to which fuel is added, *Kama* grows more and more with enjoyment and indulgence.

When the senses, the mind and intelligence are overwhelmed by Kama, the soul also gets deluded. The Gita offers a solution through the control of senses, as stated in verse 41 of Chapter III as follows:

Verse 41

Therefore, control thy desires from the beginning and slay the sinful destroyer of wisdom and discrimination.

According to the Gita, **Lust, Anger and Greed are the three gateways to Hell.** Thus *Kama* (or Lust) is placed at first place, because it can lead to both anger and greed. It follows from the above discussion that while we have to satisfy *Kama* to a desirable level, it has to be kept under constant check in order to make life useful and peaceful.

Desires in some form or shape are constantly being produced in the human mind. If one desire is satisfied, the urge to satisfy another crops up. This interplay of desires seems to be unending and only ends with the end of life. However, it again continues in the next life.

According to Indian philosophy, we should limit our desires to the barest minimum. Desires which arise out of greed, lust and anger must be curbed in our daily life. We should start with restricting desires to the level of genuine needs which have to be fulfilled, as a matter of duty. As a general rule, all unnecessary and superfluous cravings must be curbed. As all desires originate in the mind, it is in the mind that the necessary control has to be exercised. Firm mental control is essential in curbing unwanted desires. One must not yield to one's desires. Again, continuous satisfaction of desires, with a view to getting rid of them, will not end the desires. However, the suppression of desire is also not the right way, as the suppressed desires are bound to come back with greater force. The solution lies in right thinking and proper understanding of the consequences of having these desires. Strong determination and repeated reminders are helpful in ending harmful desires.

Let us consider how *Kama*, in the form of desires, plays its role in our daily life. Take the example of eating tasty, spicy food, sweets or ice creams, etc. When you eat such food for the first time, you like its taste and, therefore, like to eat such stuff again. When this process is repeated again and again, it becomes a bad habit which can create health problems. Similarly, one can develop a strong liking for other things which include sexual indulgence, craze for money, addiction to alcohol, drugs, etc. So long as desires are legitimate and kept within reasonable limits, it is all right, but when these cross the limits and become a craze, these can create considerable problems. Addiction to smoking, drinking and drugs are some of the common problems which we come across in modern times.

The urge of *Kama* arises when there is something to seek, to possess from the external world. Generally, we seek a source of comfort and pleasure, a beautiful object, which is to our liking. There is no harm in seeking and enjoying these things in a normal manner, but when we cross the reasonable limit, these desires produce greed and lust and lead to anger, disappointment and destruction.

Material desires often become a barrier which separates man from God. Therefore, desires should be cut down, reduced and eliminated altogether, if so required and possible. This would be possible if we watch our thoughts and distinguish between good and bad with the help of right understanding and wisdom. The best way to curb unnecessary desires is to direct our attention from material desires to divine desires. While desires arising out of the genuine needs of life have to be fulfilled, unwanted desires must be eliminated. In general, fulfilment of desires as a matter of duty and cultivation of noble desires which lead to common good, is of course necessary during the first two stages of life (*Brahmacharya* and *Grihastha*). The role of desires gets reduced during the third stage of *Vanprastha* and it becomes the barest minimum in the last stage (i.e. *Sanyasa*) of human life. That is why the observance of the spirit of the four stages (Ashram System) of life has great significance in Indian philosophy.

It may be relevant to mention here that the observance of principles of *Dharma*, as already described (under *Dharma*) plays a vital role in the curbing and control of unwanted and harmful desires.

●●

Moksha

Moksha is the fourth and final objective of life. It is the final goal, which implies a state of liberation from misery and pain. It is the state of 'Perfect Bliss' or *Ananda*, after attaining which nothing more remains to be attained.

This is the stage of highest purity and perfect knowledge free from all ignorance, impurities, pain and miseries of life. In this stage, the pure soul free from all blemishes and flaws, lives in a state of divine bliss.

Human life is unique. Only human beings, unlike animals and other living creatures, are endowed with higher intelligence, an ability to think, analyse and discriminate between right and wrong. In case these endowments are not used to full advantage, then there is not much difference between human and animal life.

Animals also eat, live, roam about, procreate and follow their sensual instincts. It is given to humans only that they can go beyond the animal level of existence and reach higher goals.

According to ancient Indian thought, human life is the most precious thing and therefore, should not be wasted in mundane pursuits which mainly involve gratification of senses.

The attainment of *Moksha* is the highest goal of life. That is why it is placed as the fourth or the last objective of life. There is, however, no scope for instant *Moksha*; one has to go through earlier stages and attain the first three objectives of *Dharma, Artha* and *Kama*. Our ancient Indian thought does not recommend taking of *Sanyasa* (or renunciation) from material life right from the beginning except in certain cases. Life has to be lived at the material level, from which *Artha* (wealth) has to be acquired, noble desires have to be fulfilled, but all these are required to be attained under the supervision of *Dharma*, which is the first objective of life. The need to earn wealth and the satisfaction of earthly desires and responsibilities are essential to life. But wealth and desires, *Kama* and *Artha* have to be accommodated and pursued within the overall charge of *Dharma*. Wealth has to be earned in a just manner and within a proper limit and used in proper manner. Similarly, desires have also to be kept within limits. Noble desires have to be fulfilled and bad, impure desires have to be curbed.

Earlier, we have described *Moksha*, very briefly, as the state of liberation from all pain and misery. We shall now describe this state in some greater detail. In this state, the individual soul, free from all pain and bondage of the material body, lives in the direct contact of God in a state of divine bliss. As God is present everywhere, the soul can also move around anywhere free from any hindrance. Although it is without any sense organs as in human body, yet, it has the advantage of performing all pure actions like hearing, seeing, tasting, etc. even without the physical sense organs. Thus, in this state, pure mind and five senses of knowledge keep company with the soul and can perform their respective functions for the pleasure of the soul which, however, remains free from pain. In ordinary life, the soul experiences both pleasure and pain, but in the state of *Moksha,* there is no pain; it is all pleasure or *Ananda*—the state of ultimate bliss. There is a view that after *Moksha,* the soul, ever free from birth and death, never returns to the material world again. However, there is another view contrary to it, according to which, the soul after remaining in bliss for millions of years returns to the world to resume material life again. It is not our intention here to enter into any controversy about this. The fact, however, remains that *Moksha* is the final goal of human life. This may or may not be achieved in the current span of life and may be possible only after attaining gradual progress through numerous lives. It is the most difficult objective which requires utmost purity of mind, arduous spiritual practices, constant devotion and an attitude of non-attachment. Though extremely difficult, it is not impossible. Ancient *rishis* and saints had attained this highest objective.

We will now briefly discuss how this final objective can be achieved.

●●

Means to Achieve Moksha

It is the privilege of only human beings that they can achieve the final objective of life or *Moksha* which implies liberation from all pain and misery and freedom from the bondage of birth and death. This goal is extremely difficult, but not impossible. It is believed that several saints and *rishis* have already achieved this objective.

Let us consider what happens in our real life. A child is born and he or she goes through various stages of life. During childhood and youth, he goes to school and college, where he gets education. It takes a period of 20-25 years or even more to complete education and then to enter a regular profession. It takes even more time to attain full competence in one's profession. Then he gets married, raises a family and helps them also to grow in a similar or better way. A person earns wealth and acquires all sorts of material possessions to make his life useful and comfortable. The main process of active life runs around 60-70 years, during which a person remains engrossed in fulfilling his material desires in order to gain happiness. During this present span of life, he gets good and bad experiences, pleasures and pains, name and fame, success and failure and so on, which form a vicious circle of life termed as *Maya Jaal* or the 'web of life'.

While he many succeed in getting material possessions and comforts of life, still he is lacking in complete happiness. It may not be erroneous to conclude that no one is ever happy. Pleasure and pain take their turn in the process of life. For some, it may be more pleasure while for others, more pain. However, life is always a mix of both pleasure and pain.

Our scriptures tell us that complete happiness or *Ananda* is possible on attaining *Moksha* and there are specified means to attain this stage. These means of attaining *Moksha*, as mentioned in the scriptures may be briefly stated below.

Pure Knowledge

Knowledge has been mentioned as a powerful and effective means to attain *Moksha*. It has two aspects— material and spiritual. Material knowledge gives information about the contents and benefits of material objects and how to put them into use for making our life useful and comfortable. Such knowledge which arises out of various uses of matter deals with arts and sciences and leads to various comforts and conveniences of human life. All progress and development in the world in different spheres of life is based on material knowledge.

Spiritual knowledge goes beyond matter and pertains to the Spirit—consciousness at the individual and universal level. In common language, it deals with the individual soul and God, their inter-relation, and how to know and understand them. Spiritual knowledge leads to the final Truth and its attainment, removes all ignorance, pain and misery of the bondage of human life. It takes us closer to God and leads to *Moksha*. Our scriptures, if properly understood, can act as our true spiritual guides. However, mere reading or their recitation without proper understanding their content and true meaning is of little benefit. It is essential to seek the guidance of a really learned person or a spiritual master who has really imbibed the real truth through yogic discipline, practice of *Dharma* and intense *Sadhna*.

Pure Action

Everyone in this world has to perform some action, good or bad, which leads to some consequence. There is a popular saying, 'Every action has a reaction.' Thus action and reaction produce an unending vicious circle. In human life, all actions are generally performed with a motive and in case that motive is not fulfilled, it leads to grief, pain and disappointment. All such actions lead to bondage. The Gita lays down the essential basic principles which should govern all our actions in everyday life. The core message is — *Work without concern for the result of action.* Action should be performed as a matter of duty. Action performed without attachment and without concern for consequences, with God ever in mind, in full dedication and devotion leads to liberation. Such action is pure action, or *Nishkam Karma,* and is the very basis of *Moksha.*

Pure Devotion

The third means, as mentioned in our scriptures, for attaining *Moksha* is pure devotion. It involves intense love, the highest yearning for God. Nothing else comes between a true devotee and God. However, it does not mean having blind faith or performance of foolish rituals. It does involve complete surrender to God with unflinching faith. In verse 54 of Chapter XI, the Gita says:

"By unswerving devotion to Me, O, Arjuna, I can be thus known, truly seen and entered into."

Devotion is the path of love, compassion, friendliness, non-attachment to material objects and complete purity of the mind and soul. It is love, not for things, material, etc. but love for the highest ideal. It is love, at the level of the Supreme and for his entire creation. Devotion to God is the highest and the purest form of love. A true devotee meditates on God with true love and all his actions are God-oriented. The individual's ego is destroyed by the intensity of love for God. It is the true yearning of the eager heart which seeks divine fulfilment and nothing less.

The Gita describes these means of *Moksha* in the form of three yogic disciplines of *Gyan yoga*, *Karma yoga* and yoga of devotion or *Bhakti Yoga*. However, these three means, though described separately, are not separate water– tight compartments. It is the synthesis of all these three yogas which leads to God. The practice of a particular means or path by an individual depends, by and large, upon the nature of the practitioner. In actual practice, these means cannot be practised in isolation, but all these have to be intertwined to achieve *Moksha*. The correct understanding of spiritual knowledge, performance of right actions without concern for their fruits with complete devotion and absolute surrender to God, practised together, lead to the final goal or *Moksha*.

●●

Four Stages of Human Life (Ashram Set-Up)

According to the ancient Indian philosophy, the normal span of human life has been divided into four stages. Assuming the total lifespan extending to a hundred years, each stage consists of a period of 25 years. *This division of life into four stage is known as Ashram set-up, each stage being an Ashram.* It plays a very important and effective role in the achievement of the four objectives of human life. It is necessary to understand the meaning of *Ashram* before discussing this topic in more detail. The word *Ashram* is derived from its Sanskrit root *Shram* which means 'hard labour'. It, therefore, follows that it is a period of life where hard work is required. In another sense, it also means a stage of life. According to the Indian way of thought based on Vedic philosophy, each stage of life has been associated with hard work in some form or the other. It may be work as a student to acquire education and professional skills, or struggle of a householder's life, or life of a recluse in a forest, away from home, or the final phase of a roaming *sanyasi* who lives an austere life shorn of all material possessions and their comforts.

The *Ashram* set-up assumes the lifespan consisting of hundred years. Even in Vedic prayers, one aspires to live for hundred years. On this basis, the lifespan is divided into four stages of 25 years each. However, in the present times, when the lifespan is less than hundred years, it may not be possible to strictly adhere to this division. Whatever the lifespan may be, it broadly consists of four parts or divisions which may be briefly described as follows:

Brahmacharya Ashram

This is the first stage of human life consisting of up to or around first twenty-five years of lifespan. In general, this is a period of growth and development from birth to youth and is meant for the preparation of future life. The foundation of life is laid during this period. During ancient times, boys and girls, after a particular age of childhood, were sent to the place of a teacher or *Guru* for getting education. The place for receiving such education was called *Gurukul* and used to be located away from home, in a forest area. The learned *Guru,* proficient in all aspects, would provide education to his student making shishyas follow strict discipline of a simple, austere life.

In the modern context, when the *Gurukul* system has become rather obsolete, this is the period for school, college or other professional education. The purpose remains the same or similar. It is a period for acquiring knowledge essential for living life and used as a stepping stone for subsequent stages. The student is supposed to remain unmarried and completely free from all sorts of sexual gratification. There is great stress on the conservation of vital energy in order to preserve and maintain good health of both the body and mind.

Brahmacharya is meant for acquiring all essential knowledge useful for the whole life. In fact, the firm base of all other *Ashramas* is built during this part. That is why, during this period, all essential knowledge, moral qualities, good health, professional skills, etc are required to be acquired during this *Ashram.* If the foundation is strong, the building which is being built on it will also be strong. Thus, proper observance of *Brahmacharya* is essential for all human beings.

While strict discipline required in the observance of this *Ashram* as practised in ancient times may not be possible in modern times in view of the changed perception and circumstances, it is worthwhile that the basic spirit and the fundamentals of this part of life must be kept in mind and put into practice, as far as possible. The education and qualities acquired during this stage will prove great assets for living a successful and beneficial future life.

Grihastha Ashram

Grihastha means living in a household. Accordingly, in this *Ashram,* an individual lives in a permanent residence or place, gets married, raises his family, follows a profession for livelihood and lives his life as a useful citizen of the society. It is the period for earning livelihood, acquiring wealth and property and other material objects essential for domestic life and for bringing up children, and preparing them for subsequent life. One is supposed to acquire wealth through honest and fair means. Besides running his own household, a person engages himself in other activities as well, which include social, cultural and religious spheres. A householder in this *Ashram* is supposed to lead a strictly religious life and observe various norms of moral conduct and righteousness. He is also expected to fulfil his duties and obligation towards other members of the society, as well as towards his country.

The role of providing help and service to the incumbents of the other three *Ashramas* also rests with this *Ashram.* That is why, this is the most important of all *Ashramas.* This is the source of sustenance of all other *Ashramas* and hence, occupies the most important place among all the *Ashramas*. In fact, the existence of other *Ashramas* is not possible without this *Ashram*.

Grihastha Ashram is also a period of life when an individual fulfils his various desires which include limited sexual gratification, procreation, amassing of wealth and enjoyment of the comforts of material life. But it is desirable that these enjoyments and indulgences must be kept within a reasonable, harmless limit and within the confines of moral and social discipline and restraints. Unlimited fulfilment of desires and irresponsible sensual indulgence can lead to dire consequences. Everyday increase in sexual and social crimes, rapes, murders and other scandals in public life are a pointer towards this.

Since *Grihastha Ashram* is burdened with various duties and responsibilities arising out of married life, upbringing of children, maintenance of household, social obligations, etc., the householder has to experience all the ups and downs of life. There are several obstacles which one has to face in this period which is full of struggle. One has to pass through dualities of different types which include pleasure and pain, success and failure, victory and defeat, health and disease and so on. It is a period of both pleasant and unpleasant, favourable and unfavourable situations. Great efforts and perseverance are required to face these difficult phases of life. That is why most people consider this *Ashram* as the most challenging and difficult period of life. The rigid training and discipline acquired in *Brahmacharya Ashram* are useful in facing all the odds of *Grihastha Ashram*. *Grihastha Ashram*, no doubt, is a plain field for the right practice and achievement of three main objectives of life, viz., *Dharma, Artha* and *Kama*.

In case the householder has full and right understanding of his *Dharma*, he can surely overcome all pitfalls arising out of the process of fulfilment of the next two objectives of *Artha* and *Kama*. What is required is a proper balance of fulfilment of desires and rightful duties, within the norms of practice of *Dharma*.

Vanprastha Ashram

Vanprastha Ashram constitutes the third stage of life. After having established a household, enjoyed married life, raised a family and thus, having completed all or most of the domestic responsibilities and obligations, it is now time to get away from the worldly attachments and engagements. The householder is now free to hand over the charge to the next generation. In this *Ashram*, one is supposed to leave the home and live in a forest or some other designated place, like a religious place where other such people live together and lead a simple, austere life, free from the worries of a household.

While it may not be practicable to live in a forest these days, some religious organisations have established residential devout, called *Vanprastha Ashramas*, where devout people pass through this stage of life. They utilise their time in self-study, *satsang*, performance of daily religious rituals, meditation, yogic *sadhna* and live a sort of community life among like-minded people of almost the same age group and similar mental attitude.

In this stage of life, instead of mundane desires and their fulfilment, a person devotes his time in spiritual contemplation. He may keep his wife with him or he may leave her at home under the care of his wards, as the circumstances and mutual consent may permit. However, there is no scope for any sexual gratification. A *Vanprasthic* does not have to do hard labour or take up any professional job for earning wealth. His personal needs become very limited and he leads a very simple life of spiritual pursuits.

Vanprastha is basically a period of preparation to embark upon the next and the last stage of *Sanyas*. In this period, therefore, he becomes well-versed in scriptures and acquires a spiritual bent of mind. According to the Gita, an individual should withdraw himself from sensual objects and desires, as a tortoise withdraws his limbs within him. A *Vanprasthic* has to practise this type of self-discipline on his way to achieve the higher goal of life. Having prepared himself in this manner, the practitioner of *Vanprastha Ashram* enters into the next stage of *Sanyas Ashram,* which we shall briefly describe below.

Sanyas Ashram

This is the fourth and the last stage of the *Ashram* set-up. *Sanyas* means to cast away, to relinquish. In this *Ashram,* the individual reaches the last step of the spiritual ladder after discarding all connections with his family, mundane desires and all material attachments. Such a person is a man of settled intelligence.

In other words, he is free from the liabilities of life and remains unmoved in pleasure and pain, success or failure, profit or loss and so on. Pleasant and unpleasant situations, favourable and unfavourable circumstances make no difference to a *Sanyasi* who remains the same in both the situations. A *Sanyasi* is not perturbed by painful events nor excited by comforts or pleasures for which he has no desire or longing. He is not affected by anger, fear, hatred and other similar vices.

In this *Ashram,* a *Sanyasi* acquires more and more spiritual knowledge through the constant study of scriptures and preparing himself thus, he spreads this knowledge among other members of the society for their upliftment and spiritual progress. A *Sanyasi* is not supposed to reside for a long time at one place. He lives on food stuff prepared and donated by a householder. His personal needs of food and clothing are the barest minimum. A *Sanyasi* has no expectation for any reward or fruit of his actions. He performs all actions in a spirit of detachment and accepts whatever befalls him by chance or circumstances. He is free from all vices like lust, anger, greed, false pride, hatred, jealousy and all sensual urges and inclinations. He is supposed to have become an ideal person.

It may be very pertinent to mention here that *Sanyas* is not a means to willingly escape from the responsibilities and adversities of life. It is also not a stage to seek rest and relaxation after running away from the hard realities of the life of a struggling householder. It is only after completing all his worldly responsibilities that a householder first enters into the *Vanprastha Ashram* and on its proper completion, plays the role of a *Sanyasi* where he willingly accepts and adopts the life of a wandering, desireless monk.

In the modern context, it is neither practicable nor desirable for anyone to become a *Sanyasi*, without first having acquired the requisite qualification and disciplined training for it. These days many evil-minded people masquerade as *sanyasis* in saffron robes. They are simply frauds and deceive public in the name of some or the other religion.

In general, one has to go through just two stages, i.e. *Brahmacharya* and *Grihastha,* though someone may not like these nomenclatures. One must maintain and practise the spirit behind these two *Ashramas,* though the forms may be somewhat different. Education and the life of a householder are essential in most of the cases, if not in all. Various worldly desires have to be fulfilled in *Grihastha Ashram.* But this must be done within the confines of a moral code of conduct.

In the modern context, however, it may be difficult to follow the next two *Ashramas,* i.e. *Vanprastha* and *Sanyas,* for most of the people. Even those who are able to practise these two stages of *Ashram* set-up may have to modify the time-frame to suit their actual circumstances.

While it may not be possible to strictly follow the *Ashram* set-up as envisaged in ancient times, there is no denying the fact that it provides a blueprint for living an ideal way of life for all times. We may not stick to the original form but the spirit behind its working must be upheld.

The underlying objective is to live life according to a moral code of conduct and in a well-planned manner depending upon the requirements of each stage of life and keeping in view the final goal of life, which is *Moksha.* For achieving that goal, there is no scope for a miracle or an instant formula for liberation. One has to follow a step-by-step approach and pass through all the necessary required stages of life, by whatever names these may be called. The *Ashram* set-up provides a plan in stages and a gradual approach for living life.

Thus, in the first stage, one should acquire knowledge, professional skills, physical and moral strength in order to fully prepare oneself for the subsequent stages of life.

In the second stage, he has to fulfil his worldly desires and meet his worldly aspirations and commitments through a married householder's life.

The third *Ashram* is meant to detach onself from the attachments and engagements of worldly life and thus, prepare for the last segment of life and attain the final goal of life, which is *Moksha*.

It should be amply clear from the preceding discussions, that the *Ashram* set-up provides an ideal Action Plan to live human life in a purposeful and goal-oriented manner. It is a complete package which provides for observance of *Dharma,* acquisition and expenditure of wealth, fulfilment of duties, responsibilities and noble desires and achievement of the final objective of life, i.e. *Moksha*. However, it is another matter as to how individuals make use of this plan to their advantage.

The concept of *Ashram* set-up is an extraordinary gift of Indian culture to the mankind.

●●

Role of Ashram Set-up in the Present Time

The division of human lifespan into four stages, called *Ashramas* is an ideal arrangement to live life. It was conceived and practised in ancient times. However, it is difficult to follow in actual practice in the present times, when the modes of living and demands of life have undergone a huge change. For instance, there is no place for old *Gurukuls* and the education process now starts even at a tender age of 2-3 years. However, what is really required is to follow the spirit and the motive behind this system. Therefore, necessary modifications can be made here and there to suit the needs of the present time. As the present lifespan does not really extend up to a hundred years, the period of an *Ashram* need not be confined to a strict limit of 25 years each. Even the first segment of life which is meant for getting education may extend beyond 25 years and so on.

As the last segment is full of penance and hard life, one is required to be physically fit and mentally well-equipped, aided by spiritual background and inclination in order to enter the *Sanyas Ashram*. It may also not be feasible to live in a forest or keep wandering from place to place as a mendicant. In the present set-up, one may practise *Sanyas* even in the household, although this may not be an ideal arrangement as enjoined in our scriptures. In *Sanyas,* what really matters is the right mental attitude, the spirit of sacrifice, a desireless, detached mode of living and an irresistible longing to reach the final goal of life. In spite of difficulties inherent in the observance of the *Ashram* set-up in its original form, it has an important role to play even in present times, by making necessary modifications here and there, as required in view of the prevailing circumstances. However, the underlying philosophy and the right mental attitude must prevail. If this is done, then for a common man, it may not be necessary to leave the household to go to a forest, as it is not really practicable to do so in the last two stages of life.

●●

Some Helpful Aids

We have already mentioned the three basic means to achieve the final objective of *Moksha*. The following requisites and practices may be helpful in this process:

GOOD HEALTH

As the path to liberation is extremely arduous, it is essential to maintain good health, both physical and mental. There is a direct relation between our body and mind. A healthy body is supposed to have a healthy mind. A healthy body and healthy mind are useful even for attaining material progress; these are much more necessary for spiritual attainments. A body, free from any disease or infirmity is a great blessing. Good vegetarian balanced food, proper regular exercise in an unpolluted environment and pure and positive thoughts are very helpful in maintaining good health. One must follow all the required principles and practices which lead to good health—both of the physical body and the mind. Simple muscular exercises, physical postures in the form of suitable Yogic *Asanas,* brisk regular walking, etc. are some of the easily available options.

PRANAYAM

Pranayam as a means for the regulation of breathing process is an ancient remedy for the proper maintenance of physical and mental health. It is very useful for concentration and control of mind and helps in meditation and yogic *sadhna.* It is the key to the path of achieving higher consciousness and should be practised in a right and regular manner. It is an effective means for the purification of mind.

The correct method of practising *pranayam* should be learned from a qualified and experienced yoga practitioner.

MEDITATION

It is a very important and essential aid for attaining progress in the path of liberation. Through long and regular practice of meditation, it is possible to achieve the state of pure consciousness. It is a positive means of self-purification and spiritual progress.

However, a proper background in spiritual awareness is necessary for success in achieving good results. Awareness of the percept of God, full knowledge of His attributes and functioning and complete surrender to the will of God are some of the basic conditions for fruitful meditation. While different methods for practising meditation may be available these days, a devotee may do well by learning and perfecting one which is most suitable to him.

PRAYER

It is the channel of communication with the Supreme; it is the opening of one's inner consciousness to the universal consciousness. In simple words, it is an individual effort to meet God and show devotion. Prayer demands selfless love, sincerity and complete unswerving faith in God. It is pure love for the Supreme, without any selfish motive, reward or material expectation—this mode is the best form of prayer. What really matters is the attitude of the mind behind prayer.

One must pray regularly and sincerely for a long time, before one can succeed in establishing a close relationship with God.

SWADHYAY

It implies study of scriptures and other good literature written by saints, seers and genuine spiritual teachers and thinkers. It also includes listening to spiritual discourses, etc. There is another meaning which points to the study of the self or self-analysis. An aspirant must constantly keep analysing positive and negative tendencies of the mind, discriminate between the right and wrong, and thus, gradually keep progressing on the spiritual path.

Mere reading and reciting from religious books without proper understanding is not *Swadhyay*. Besides understanding the contents, one must imbibe the spirit of what has been read and practise the knowledge so gained in everyday life. Thus, it should be a real, purposeful exercise in self-education and progress.

Repeated and regular study of good literature written by inspiring guides brings improvement in thoughts and actions. *Swadhyay* is a great help in removing ignorance and paves the way to right knowledge and proper understanding of one's enviorment.

As good food is essential for good health of the physical body, *Swadhyay* is beneficial for the proper nourishment of the mind and the soul. It acts like a tonic and must be undertaken regularly for both material and spiritual progress.

SATSANG

Listening to religious discourses, religious songs, in a religious place with a group of religious people in an organised manner, is called *Satsang*. *Satsang* literally means 'the company of God'. Devotional practices which include prayer meetings, group meditation, etc. are parts of a Satsang.

The discourses provide knowledge about God, His attributes, besides teachings of holy saints and scriptures. They tell us about the purpose of life and how it can be achieved. Regular attendance of *Satsang* can have a healthy effect on the mind and can remove ignorance. Thus, it paves the way for spiritual progress.

Keeping company of good people and reading of good literature are also forms of *Satsang*. At the individual level, *Satsang* can make a person righteous. At the level of society, it provides a forum for fellowship and even service to the society, in some form or the other. Thus, a *Satsang* is a good aid for spiritual development.

CHARITY

Charity is a divine virtue which is also a useful social activity. It means giving something useful to the needy and deserving people, which include orphans, widows, the disabled, poor and sick people etc., who depend upon outside financial help. Charity can be offered in the form of money and also articles. It may be cash, food, medicines, clothing and other utility items. Now a days, even organs of the body (like eye, kidney, etc.) can be donated. We can extend charity even to the sick and hungry animals, birds, etc., who need our assistance and kindness.

Charity should be shown only to the deserving people, at the right time and place. It should not be offered to the rich, the killers, criminals and other unsocial elements. Charity should be practised in word, thought and deed. Sometimes, even a word of sympathy brings cheer to the sick person.

Charity is useful both for the giver and the taker. It brings joy, satisfaction and peace to both the parties and is a very desirable practice for spiritual development.

ASHTANG YOGA

Ashtang Yoga is the perfect discipline to attain *Moksha*. Maharishi Patanjali, the author of *Yoga Sutra* or *Yoga Darshan,* a treatise on yoga, is the founder of Ashtang Yoga. It consists of eight parts, which are *Yamas, Niyamas, Asana, Pranayam, Pratihara, Dharma, Dhyana* and *Samadhi.* During *Samadhi,* which is the last stage of *Ashtang Yoga,* the individual's soul experiences communion with the Supreme soul. This is the stage of *Moksha*—liberation from birth and death, pain and misery. The eight parts of *Ashtang Yoga* are briefly described as follows:

I. YAMAS

There are five *Yamas,* which are in the nature of social obligations or restraints. These may be briefly described as follows:

1. AHIMSA (Non-violence): *Ahimsa* means absence of violence in thought, word and deed. In the broad sense, it means to treat all beings with love and without anger, hatred and injustice. It involves elimination of all evil thoughts and enmity of all types. As a general rule, one must abstain from unnecessary and uncalled for violence in all aspects of life.

2. SATYA (Truth): It has a spiritual connection. God is truth or truth is God. In day-to-day life, truth means to speak or write of a thing and believe it to be so, as it really is. One should first establish the reality, then accept and believe it and thereafter, follow in action. One should not think, speak and act differently.

3. ASTEYA (Non-stealing): In general, it means non-stealing. To take away something unjustly, deceitfully or without the permission of the owner is *Steya* and not to do so is *Asteya.* One has to cultivate the attitude of *Asteya* in actual working life.

4. BRAHMACHARYA (Celibacy or regulation of sexual impulses): It means celibacy and maintenance of a strict discipline in sexual indulgence. One may not marry at all, and thus remain a celebate throughout one's life. In case of married life, one may strictly regulate his sex life by associating only with his wife. His sexual relation with wife also has to be well-regulated and limited. There has to be a complete control over one's sexual urges both in thought and deed. It also means to tread on the path which leads to God. Thus, following right conduct is an essential part of *Brahmacharya*.

5. **APARIGRAHA** The general meaning of *Parigraha* is to acquire, to procure, to accumulate, etc. One may acquire wealth, property and other material objects. *Aparigraha* is the opposite of *Parigraha*. It is natural and necessary to acquire the necessities of life in order to maintain a household etc. but this should be kept within proper limit. While our genuine requirements have to be met, desires should not become necessities. It is undesirable to accumulate beyond actual requirements. Greed should not rule over our genuine requirements.

NIYAMAS

Five *Niyamas* form the second part of *Ashtang Yoga*. These are in the nature of personal discipline. *Yamas* and *Niyamas* both combined constitute personal and social code of conduct. The five *Niyamas* are as follows:

1. SHAUCHA (Cleanliness): This is of two types — external and internal. External *Shaucha* means cleanliness of the body and physical environment. Internal *Shaucha* includes purity of mind, intellect, thoughts and feelings. All negative feelings, evil thoughts such as ignorance, lust, greed, anger, false pride etc. should be avoided. Purity of mind is essential for spiritual development.

2. SANTOSHA (Contentment): It implies absence of desire to possess more of the necessities of life than are necessary for its preservation. One should work honestly to one's ability and full capacity and be satisfied with the result of efforts, whatever it may be. However, it does not mean laziness. It also does not mean that one should resign to fate and make no efforts. It means making all efforts and then be satisfied with what you get. It is said that contentment is the greatest wealth.

3. TAPA (Austerity): It is the capacity to face all odds in the performance of *Dharma*. It implies that one should have the fortitude to remain calm in the face of opposites of life, such as heat and cold, loss and gain, pleasure and pain etc. It is the capacity to face all difficulties bravely. However, it does not mean infliction of pain to the body, as a religious ritual, under some wrong belief or blind faith.

4. SWADHYAY: We have already covered it separately.

5. ISHWARA PRANIDHAN [Surrender to God]: It means total dedication of all actions to God. Full faith and pure devotion are implied. It implies full acceptance and resignation to the will of God. A person, who practises *Ishwara Pranidhan* in thought, word and deed, experiences love and grace of God and achieves divine bliss.

ASANA [Posture for meditation]: This is the third part of the *Ashtang Yoga*. It prepares a practitioner for meditation by enabling him to keep the body in a position where he can sit still with back erect for a long time. It is essential to keep the body under control before attempting to control the mind. There are several *Asana* and their variations but these are physical exercises to keep the body fit. For the purpose of meditation, a stable and comfortable sitting posture of the body is called *Asana*. This is the posture in which one should feel at ease for a reasonable long period of time. Thus, *Asana* is an essential requirement for the practice of yoga discipline.

PRATYAHARA [Withdrawal of senses]: The senses are outward looking and and it is necessary to restrain them and to train them to look inwards. This process of withdrawal of senses is called *Pratyahara,* through which senses follow the mind which gets focused inside. Thus, concentration on the desired object or idea becomes easy and the mind follows the right track to pass the next stage of the yogic discipline.

DHARANA: When the mind and the senses get focused inward, then it becomes possible to focus the mind on one point or object or idea. Such focusing of the mind is called *Dharana* in which the mind becomes stable and at peace, free from outside distractions.

DHYANA: When the state of *Dharana* gets established and continues like a flow of consciousness in one direction, then the state of *Dhyana* is ushered in. In this state, the entire concentration is on a single point. The mind becomes silent, still and motionless.

SAMADHI: This is the last stage of the *Ashtang Yoga* and is the culmination of yoga. In *Dhyana,* the aspirant is ardently in search of the object of his realisation. In *Samadhi,* the object comes into his direct experience. This is actually the stage of God-realisation or *Moksha.*

Ashtang Yoga and its eight parts have been briefly described above. An aspirant has to fully understand and grasp these sections before embarking upon their full-fledged practice. It is necessary to seek guidance from an adept or a genuine teacher of the Yoga discipline. The practice and mastery of *Ashtang Yoga* is a sure means to attain *Moksha.*

Note: For knowing more details of *Ashtang Yoga* please read the book entitled 'ESSENCE OF MAHARISHI PATANJALI'S ASHTANG YOGA' by the same author published by PUSTAK MAHAL.

●●

Epilogue

$\mathscr{H}$uman life is unique and has a definite goal which can be achieved even in the present span of life by pursuing a planned and disciplined path based on moral values. The role of *Dharma* (True religion or righteousness) is supreme in this process. In such a purposeful life, one has to achieve some essential objectives by following an action plan based on *Dharma, Artha, Kama* and *Moksha*. The final objective of *Moksha* or liberation is to be attained through the proper fulfilment of the first three objectives of *Dharma, Artha* and *Kama*.

First of all, one must know, understand and practise *Dharma* which forms the first fundamental objective. It should prevail in all aspects of life. It is the prime pursuit which influences and moulds all other pursuits of life. In short, *Dharma* means 'just and impartial moral conduct.'

The acquisition of *Artha* or wealth is the second objective of life as it is essential for living a good life.

But wealth must be procured through fair and honest means and should be used for noble and desirable purposes. It should also be kept within a proper limit without any lust and greed attached to it.

The third objective of life is the fulfilment of noble desires in a disciplined and well-regulated manner. Desires must be kept and fulfilled within a proper limit, with the thought of God always in mind.

The principles of *Dharma* must be observed and practised in the acquisition of *Artha* and fulfilment of all desires (*Kama*).

Moksha is the final objective of human life. There is no instant *Moksha*. One has to pass through and achieve the first three objectives of *Dharma, Artha* and *Kama* before attaining the final objective, i.e. *Moksha*.

●●

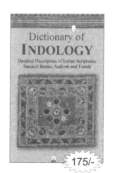

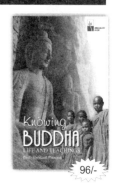

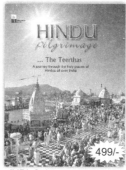
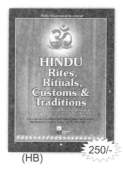

More shades of Hinduism

Krishna — The God Who Lived as Man
Bhawana Somaaya
350/-
(HB)

Echoes of **Ancient Indian Wisdom**
The Universal Hindu Vision and Its Edifice
295/-
(HB)

Bhrigu Samhita
295/-
(HB)

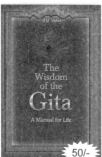

The Wisdom of the **Gita** — A Manual for Life
50/-

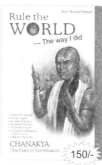

Rule the **WORLD** — The way I did
CHANAKYA The Guru of Governance
150/-

Krishna
195/-
(HB)

BHAJA GOVINDAM
An insight into Sahaja Japa Yoga
60/-

Know the **Vedas** At a Glance
80/-

I'm proud to be a **HINDU**
195/-

Postage Rs. 25/- per book. Rs. 10/- extra for each additional book

Available at all leading bookstores or
log on to our online bookstore www.pustakmahal.com

More shades of Hinduism

96/-

120/-

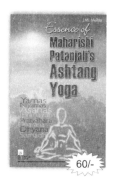

60/-

96/-

80/-

160/-

80/-

150/-

96/-

Postage Rs. 25/- per book. Rs. 10/- extra for each additional book

Available at all leading bookstores or
log on to our online bookstore www.pustakmahal.com

More shades of Hinduism

80/-

80/-

80/-

96/-

80/-

80/-

80/-

60/-

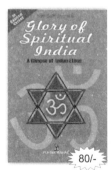

80/-

Postage Rs. 25/- per book. Rs. 10/- extra for each additional book